The Totnes Col

Bill Bennett

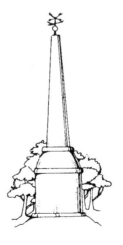

OBELISK PUBLICATIONS

PLATE ACKNOWLEDGEMENTS

I would like to thank The Totnes Museum Society for giving me the freedom to select photographs from their collection. I would also like to thank Nicholas Horne for pages 5, 13, 16, 23, 32, 43, 44, 54, 56, 58 and 61; Eric Morrison for pages 7, 38, 39, 46, 53, and the back cover.

Other Obelisk Publications

AROUND & ABOUT THE HALDON HILLS, Chips Barber
THE LOST CITY OF EXETER, Chips Barber
DIARY OF A DARTMOOR WALKER, Chips Barber
ADVENTURE THROUGH RED DEVON, R B Cattell
AN EXETER BOYHOOD, Frank Retter
UNDER SAIL THROUGH SOUTH DEVON, R B Cattell
IDE, Bill Rowland
DIARY OF A DEVONSHIRE WALKER, Chips Barber
RAMBLING IN PLYMOUTH, Woolley & Lister
GREAT LITTLE DARTMOOR BOOK, Chips Barber
GREAT LITTLE EXETER BOOK, Chips Barber
DEVONAIR BOOK OF FAMILY WALKS, Chips Barber
RUNNING IN DEVON, John Legge
MEMORIES OF NEWTON ABBOT, Elsie Townsend
CREDITON COLLECTION, Albert Labbett

HAUNTED HAPPENINGS IN DEVON, Judy Chard
MADE IN DEVON, Chips Barber & David FitzGerald
DARTMOOR IN COLOUR, Chips Barber
BURGH ISLAND AND BIGBURY BAY, Chips Barber & Judy Chard
DARK & DASTARDLY DARTMOOR, Sally and Chips Barber
TALKING ABOUT TOPSHAM, Sara Vernon
AN ALPHINGTON ALBUM, Pauline Aplin & Jeanne Gaskell
PICTURES OF PAIGNTON, Peter Tully
TALES OF THE UNEXPLAINED, Judy Chard
EXETER IN COLOUR, Chips Barber
TORBAY IN COLOUR, Chips Barber
THE DAWLISH COLLECTION, Bernard Chapman

First Published in 1989 by Obelisk Publications, 2 Church Hill, Pinhoe, Exeter, Devon
Designed by Chips Barber, Typset by Sally Barber
Printed in Great Britain by Penwell Ltd, Parkwood, Callington, Cornwall.
© Bill Bennett 1989
All Rights Reserved

The Civic Procession for the Proclamation of the Accession of King George V in 1910. The town's two silver gilt maces carried by the Macebearers were presented to the town in 1759 by Sir Richard Lloyd one of the two MPs for the Borough. In 1867, when a Reform Bill defranchised the town, only one Member of Parliament was returned.

4

Opposite left

General Sir Wm. R. Birdwood (famous First World War soldier) received the Freedom of the Borough on 21 August 1919. Later he became a Field Marshal and was created Lord Birdwood of Totnes and Anzac. The Birdwood family has been connected with the county over several centuries

Opposite right

On this very important and auspicious occasion the Borough Council are seen in procession in the Fore Street, in June 1953. Cllr. E. S. Nott was the Mayor at the time. The celebrations were to mark the Coronation of Queen Elizabeth II.

Right

This is an old photograph of the 16th century Guildhall, a grey stone building of great character and distinction. In 1749 the bell hung in the 'tower', originally the bell of the Maudlyn or Leper Hospital, was given to the King Edward VI Grammar School and used until 1966. The bell is now at the Museum.

Warland is seen here decorated for the Coronation celebrations of King George VI and Queen Elizabeth in 1937.

Two monarchs have visited Totnes, Charles I and Elizabeth II. Charles I came in September 1625 and found the town in a very festive spirit. The King and his retinue were greeted by an oration from Mr Campion and the King given a "fair purse" containing two hundred pounds. Everyone then attended a feast where 23 and a half gallons of sack were consumed and eight gallons of claret wine - there was no breathaliser test for the cavaliers! However, after the visit there was much discontent - the Mayor, Robert Gwyne, records in his accounts various objections to the expenses! The Corporation would not defray the costs of the visit and dipping into private pockets had to take place to pay for the ceremonies. This photograph shows the Queen and Prince Philip outside the Parish Church in July 1962 with a Guard of Honour of the 2nd Company, Totnes Boys Brigade. Also in the photograph is their captain (W. Howard), the vicar of Totnes (Reverend Gordon H Samuel) and the Mayor and Mayoress (Douglas and Leila Mitchell). This Royal visit ensured a toilet being provided for the first time in the ancient Guildhall - a great relief to the Town Council!

7

Street parties for Royal Celebrations have always been traditional and popular. This party took place at Warland in 1953 for the Coronation of Queen Elizabeth II. The Mayor, Cllr. Ernest Nott, and his wife Cissie are present. Ernest Nott inherited Veasey's the printers of High Street.

The Church Walk, or Exchange, which formerly stood in the High Street in front of the Parish Church was given to the Town in 1616 by Richard Lee. In token of gratitude, the Town presented his two daughters with enamelled gold rings - the Town Museum displays the ring presented to Lee's married daughter, Catherine Luscombe. Richard Lee was Mayor in 1603, and he was a great benefactor to the town. His benefactions included those to help poor children in good craft and science and later more for placing poor children to Masters as apprentices - also a resident preacher was provided for. The Church Walk was erected in 1611 by Richard Martyn on part of the Parish churchyard and donated five years later by Richard Lee. One of the granite pillars has Richard inscribed on it and another Lee. The building was rebuilt in 1719 and taken down in 1878. Some of the pillars including the inscribed ones, now stand outside the Guildhall.

This shows the interior of Totnes Parish Church which was restored by the architect Sir Gilbert Scott in 1867. The stone screen dates from 1459 and the candelabra of pure English brass from 1701. The Parish Church provides a landmark and its 120 foot high pinnacled tower can be seen from a great many miles away.

These are the Totnes Parish Church Bellringers of 1925 and include Jim Brown, F. W. Nott, Bill Fort and Bill Stephens.

Here the Totnes Borough Council are assembled for the Mayor making of Cllr. Robert Drennan in 1925/6. The Town Clerk (George Windeatt) is seen talking to his cousin Lt. Col. Frank Windeatt. The Windeatt family have been prominent in the Town over the centuries. Windeatt's solicitors were established in the 19th century. The young man in the photo, Edward Windeatt, is still the Head of the Family Firm.

Here Mrs F Rowe, Mayoress, can be spied launching the Racing shell "Totnes Pride" in 1948. Also pictured are Miss Rowe, Headmistress of Grove School, John Luscombe, Bill and Mrs Phillips and Jack Bowyer. Dart ARC have proudly existed as a club for well over 100 years.

In the notes of the Totnes Antiquarian Society 25 March 1920, there is a reference to a paper on the Colson and Langdon Bequest to repair the breach in Totnes Weir in 1703. There had been two separate breaches in the weir as well as that in the bank of the leat about 1894, when the Fish House was washed away and considerable damage done. Formerly in connection with the Mill property, there were two fishing traps in the sluices, one at the weir and the other where the Bacon Factory now stands. They were let at £80 a year, and were then the property of the charity trustees. However, this right of fishing was taken away by Act of Parliament. The Tithe Map of 1840, for Littlehempston, shows the Fish House. It also shows that the tide flowed up river as high as the weir at a time when the parish boundaries were different. A cottage called Weir Cottage is shown, on or near the same site, on the 6 inch OS map of 1890.

14

This view of the River Dart waterfront shows the 1907 Totnes Landing Stage, mid 19th century warehouses, Totnes Bridge (1828) and the Island. The steamer fares to Dartmouth were 2/6d return and 1/6d single, cycles 1/- and motor cycles 2/- each way. "Boats For hire" without a man 6d - 1s per hour, or 5s per day; with a man it was 1/6d for the first hour, 1s per hour after. Those were the days!

This shows the Annual Inspection of the River Dart by the Dart Harbour Navigation Commissioners and invited guests in 1969. (L to R) F. Brunsdon (Chairman Totnes RDC), J. Marshford (Mayor of Dartmouth), R. Niles (Chairman Dart Navigation Commissioners), A.J. Brook (affectionately known, as 'Togo ', surveyor to the commissioners and a great authority on the River), W. Bennett (Mayor of Totnes), and A. Reeves (Managing Director, Reeves Timber Ltd., Totnes).

16

Totnes, The Big Tree.

This was the big 'chestnut' tree which stood for some centuries near to the wall of the Seymour Hotel and close to Pathfields and Steamer Quay Road. It gave immense joy to Totnesians but alas it became dangerous and was felled in the mid 1950s. A Japanese flowering cherry tree took its place - but "oh for the English Chestnut"!

This is how Totnes Plains looked at the turn of the century - a wide street on the west bank of the River Dart. The elegant Town houses were built in the early 19th century and later in the century were taken over for commercial purposes necessitating a special railway branch line to and from Totnes Station .

Portland House (which was next to the Royal Seven Stars) was let at the "turn of century' in superior apartments, but eventually became 'ye Old Oak Cafe'. The building was demolished in 1936 to make way for the Coronation Road.

This 'country scene' was by the Bacon Factory just before the construction of the Coronation Road 1936 - Manor House can be seen on the right.

20

This picture of inter war development shows the works construction of Coronation Road (1936) breaking through from Ye Old Oak Cafe on the Plains to a point in front of the Bacon factory and continuing on to link up with Station Road in front of Baldwin's Garage.

This is Baldwin's Garage which was founded in 1920. In 1922, after the original premises were found to be too small, up to date works were erected in Station Road. Tommy Baldwin (engineer), Head of the Firm, had worked with Thorneycrofts at Basingstoke. The petrol pump was one of just a few in the district, (Baldwin's were agents for Morris Motors). The whole of the electric current used for lighting and power for the machinery was generated by a two kilowatt plant, complete with storage battery. There was a main switchboard - the telephone number was Totnes 51. A large number of batteries were charged for wirelesses and there were also lock up garages which had electric light and there was the showroom at 44 Fore Street.

For more than 100 years, up until the late 1940's Symonds Cider had a works on Totnes Plains. Much of the local apple crop was brought in by horse and wagon or on the special railway branch line which ran from the main station across the Plains to the timber wharf on the River Dart. Messrs. Phillips & Luscombe were familiar and popular figures with their horses.

The Horse Fairs took place on the Plains and were were held in May and October. Stalls selling sweets, umbrellas, harnesses, brushes and other items were much in evidence and there were swing boats and other entertainments for the young.

Totnes Races are alleged to have commenced in 1785 and ended in 1939. They were traditionally a two day meeting held in September. The course was a tough one by modern steeplechasing standards. It ran across fields and rivers and around Bourton Hall and down the main Newton Abbot road for a mile. This was followed by a sharp turn into the River Dart again, and back on the race course to run on towards the winning post. It was a major calendar event in the Town and was attended by thousands. During the Second World War the course next to the Dart was used by the Americans to build barges for the D-Day landings. Unfortunately the ground was never suitable for racing after that and became an industrial estate.

In the far left photograph we can see where the mid Victorian Bridgetown Church was gutted by fire, caused by a vagrant, on 9 July 1976. It was later re-consecrated by the Lord Bishop of Exeter and the Patron, the Duke of Somerset, on 10 May 1980. The next picture opposite shows Len Beer assisting the Police in fighting the fire of the Market Hall, now the site of the Civic Hall, on 17 March 1955. The South Street wall and Masonic Lodge can be seen in the background. The photograph on this page shows the general scene at the Market Hall fire.

Another great fire in January 1903 involved the destruction of Hayman & Sons (wholesale & retail drapers), Mrs Melton's (drapery & ladies' outfitting), Mr E.B. Stoyle's (boot & shoe shop), F. J. Reeves (coal office and private dwelling house), and Nos. 36, 38, 40 and 42 High Street. The cause of the fire was due to a piece of ribbon hitting a gas jet in the window of Messrs. Hayman's. The fire raged for several hours and brigades from Paignton and Exeter arrived to assist the Totnes Fire Brigade. Under Captain H.T. Distin they fought bravely to control the fiery furnace. At one time an upper wall crashed and stunned Fireman F. Seaford, one of the first firemen to have arrived on the scene. The whole of the centre of the town, including the Butterwalk, was in constant danger. The fire engine took 15 minutes to get up steam and a special train brought the Exeter brigade within an hour - three cheers for the GWR!

This splendid photograph was taken on June 26, 1902 - a few months before the great fire caused so much destruction.

This is a bus of the Devon Motor Transport Company and is seen on the Plains in May 1925. (L to R) C. Evans, M. Gould, P.V. Barber and C. Cross. The Western National Co came to Totnes in 1936, and provided Totnesians with an invaluable service.

With the advent of motor transport during and after the First World War, 'charabanc outings' became extremely popular. This charabanc is outside the Steam Packet Inn in the 1920s - the small girl standing in the front is Dorothy Collings (nee King) of St Peter's Quay.

Until recently the lower parts of Totnes have always been vulnerable to flooding, particularly when prolonged spells of continuous rain combined with high spring tides to inundate the Plains, Warland and Malt Mill areas. Sometimes the water was deep enough to stall the engines of the Western National buses. Fortunately a flood prevention scheme has alleviated this watery problem.

Prosperity to the
Worthey Town
of Totnes

Many locals will not know of the existence of the Totnes Teapot (1768) which is in Leeds Ware brown and white speckled glaze and is owned and exhibited by the FitzWilliam Museum, Cambridge. It stands 10 inches tall and is 14 inches from handle to spout!

Seen here in May 1936 are the staff of the Western National Bus Co. at their new garage in Ticklemore Street which was demolished for flats in 1988. The photo includes such well known characters as Arthur Gloyns, Bert Waring, Dick Bolt, Frank Narramore, Charlie Stuart, Jack Shillabear, Ted Newcombe, Alfie Fice, J. Blake, G. Mason, Frank Wreford, Jack Payne and Charlie Haley.

This was the first Totnes Ambulance, in the mid 1920s - a converted Model T Ford belonging to the Order of St John and the British Red Cross. It was dedicated in the mews of the Royal Seven Stars Hotel. The vehicle was provided and maintained by Harrison's Garage. On the left is Arnold Wheatley (Manager Midland Bank, Treasurer), next to him is Ambulance Officer John Walker (Manager, Boots Chemist), third from left Charles Niles (Chairman - Director of Harrison's Garage) and extreme right is Medical officer Dr. Bowes, a general practitioner in Bridgetown.

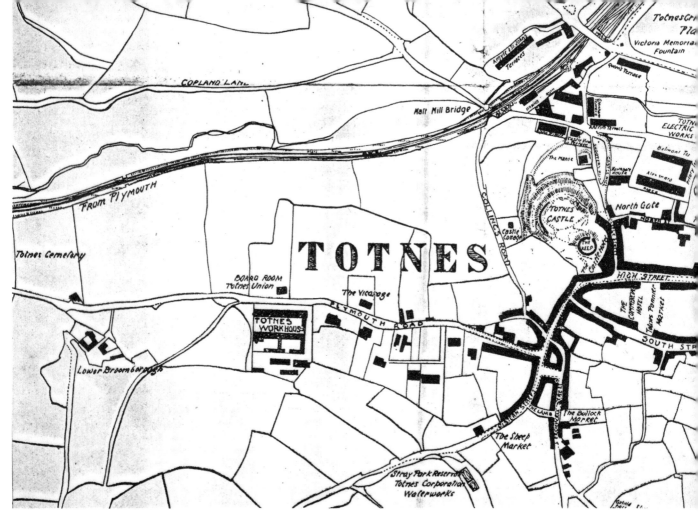

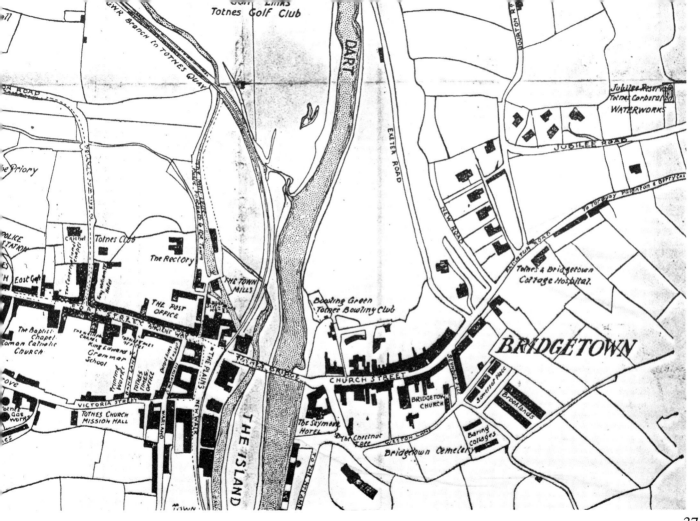

Totnes carnivals were held in November until 1924 when the view was that a summer carnival would be better for the young people. Totnes Carnival continues to this day as one of the largest in the area. The crowning of the Queen and the dancing of the Floral Dance through the streets and alleyways of the town, for many years, were the highlights of the carnival week.

One year in the grand procession the Totnes Queen's float became jammed under the East Gate because of its height - causing some delay and embarrassment to the host town!

In the business entries there was always friendly rivalry between the two florists G. Heath and Son and J. Gill & Son. Their magnificent floral tableaux on topical themes were always a highlight of the procession.

In 1951 Totnes made a notable contribution to the Festival of Britain celebrations. A two and a half hours pageant, with 600 townsfolk participating and a schoolchildren's choir of 300, was performed for a week in the grounds of the castle. The pageant was written by Frances Mace and Alan Gibson. The Pageant was directed by Harry Grinder and the narrator was Bernard Reed. The photo shows the Civil War in Totnes and amongst the Cavaliers were Jack and Will Todd. The Todd Family were noted for their singing and sporting expertise. The Roundheads had Jack Tucker and Jack Tebbutt amongst them whilst Eric Keat sat in front with his dog.

Here we have the Totnes Guide Company on parade for Youth Empire Sunday, 22 May 1955 and led by their Guide Captain, Miss R. Windeatt. Behind on the Captain's left is Guide Leader June Prowse (nee Mills) and on her right Lt. Doris Turner.

Totnes King Edward VI Grammar School was founded in 1553. The school's original premises adjoined the Guildhall and 20 boys attended. In 1887 when the number of boys had increased and education had become available for everyone the school moved to an elegant Georgian mansion in Fore Street. The school remained there until moving to the new King Edward VI comprehensive school on the Redworth site in 1971. The 6th forms also moved to that site some years later and the Mansion is now used for community education. This photograph shows the tree planting on the Governors' field at Weirfields 31 October 1953 to celebrate the 400th anniversary of the school's foundation.

Here are the staff of Redworth Secondary Modern School, Totnes in 1953. (Standing back row L to R) Messrs. Downes, Owen, Barber, Voss, Langford, Parker, Richardson, Taylor, Cumberland and Roberts. (Sitting L to R) Miss Knapman, Mrs Postle, Mr Blight, Mr Jeffery (headmaster), Miss Clive, Mrs Whitehead and Mrs Hartridge. Mr Jeffery took over as the first Headmaster of Redworth school on 10 January 1939, then called the Totnes Senior Council School. He had previously been headmaster of Buckfastleigh Council School. He retired on 31 March 1953 and was succeeded by Mr J. Rundle.

Totnes County School for Girls, opened Jan. 19th 1928.

Totnes County School for Girls was opened on 19 January 1928 by Mrs Oxley Durrant Parker of Sharpham House. It cost £10,000 and Miss A.M.E. Scott MA was the headmistress.

Here Michael Bennett (pupil of Redworth School) is seen asking for the traditional Mayor's holiday in 1956 from the Mayor H. B. Reed (also a schoolmaster at Redworth School). The Town Sergeant, for many years Jim Maddick, can be seen resplendent in uniform. The lady (far right) is Lilley Ramsden who was the first Lady Mayor of Totnes 1945/6. The asking by pupils from the schools of Totnes for a Mayor's holiday has for generations been a highlight of the ancient Mayor Choosing ceremony in the Tudor Guildhall. The first Mayor of Totnes dates back to 1359 and the Mayoral Boards name all the Mayors from that date. The Choosing was, for many centuries, in November but was changed to May. At the Mayor's Banquet the 17th Loving Cup is used for the (ancient) Toast "Unanimity and Prosperity to the Town of Totnes and success to the Trade thereof". If the toast is not said correctly a fine is imposed by the Town Sergeant for the Mayor's charity - the word unanimity is not the easiest of words to pronounce in our language after a convivial meal!

46

In 1919 many residents and the Borough Council talked of the need for a Park to be used as a recreation ground. Eventually, when ground from the Stearts Estate was on the market, land was purchased for a Borough Park. This photo shows a Band Stand and palm trees on the Borough Park which have since gone.

The cost of the bowling green laid was less than £300. Its inaugural opening match, on 15 June 1928, took place between Totnes and Dawlish Clubs - Dawlish being the winners. The Totnes team consisted of: F.G. Edgcumbe, A. Mulhall, H. Kird, E.G. Head, R. N. Armstrong, A.S. Robertson, C. Hulland, J. S. Brook, G. Dowell, S. J. Veasey, H. J.Collins, W. Beer, E. B. Stoyle, E. W. Hayman, D. Fletcher, W. Evans, G. B. French, E. Samuel, F. Horn and C.H. Wellington.

Totnes Youth Hostel A.F.C. 1939-1940. (Back row) A. Brown, A. Beer (committee members), C. Maddock, J. Congdon, Rev. O. L. Willmott, D. Potter, W. T. Wyatt (capt.), F. W. Tucker (hon. sec.), P. Hannaford (trainer). (Middle row) D. Rowe, L. V. Trivett, W. Skedgwell, P. F. St John, L. Boyes. (Front row) L. R. Wickett (vice capt.), C. F. Rice, R. Murch, D. Owen.

This fine young body of men represented Totnes A.F.C. in the 1948-1949 season.

Totnes Cricket Club, 1954. (Back row L to R) Stan Murch, Gilbert Davies, Dean Davies, David Lee, George Stevens, Roy Stabb, John Hodge and Brian Horrell, (middle) Eleanor Coish (front row) Ken Coish, Bob Murch, Les Downs, Doug Perry and Alf Hooker.

Totnes RFC 1961-2 (Back row L to R) Jack Arscott, Norman Inglis, Billy Osborne, Stan Hannaford, Godfrey Horsman, Frank Vallance, Sid Rowe, Vic Parnel and Peter Perring OBE (middle row) Roy Stabb, Brian Perring, Mike Mingo, Toby Finch, George Westaway (Capt.), David Manning and Les Lang (front row) John Edworthy, Paul Evans, David Thatcher, John Howrihane, John Crout and Melvyn Prowse.

The Totnes Swimming Club Party of February 1956 was held at the affectionately known "Tin Tab", Bridgetown. Amongst the Party are Dot Ramsden, Mary Long, Dorothy Hatch, Eileen Skewis, David Wilkinson, Douglas Morrison and Derek Rowe.

These fine young people were members of the Totnes Weirhead Swimming Club (1930s). Efforts were going ahead then for a swimming pool but the dream was not realised until 1977 - Cllr. C. Blake (past Mayor) being one of those instrumental in resolving the problem. Members included Courtney Blake standing second L to R at back, and Len Horswill (4th from L sat in front). Adults seated in front were Mr C. Bow, Mr Powney and Mrs Foale.

The 1927 1st Totnes Troop of Scouts which had existed for many years endured a minor crisis when it lost its Scoutmaster and had to be disbanded after several months. The Rev. L. Conty built up the new troop - the 2nd Totnes Group - and meetings were held at the Church Mission Hall. Dartington Woods were used for outdoor scouting. The photo shows 'Pop' Rowlands, District Commissioner, leading a Camp Fire on the Island. The young man with the Sea Scout Cap is Rendle Crang who for many years has been the Sea Scout Group Leader and, more recently, Mayor of Totnes.

Opposite left

During the Second World War Totnesians helped the War effort. Wooden minesweepers were built on the Baltic Wharf, whilst the engines were installed at Dartmouth. Many men and women were employed on this secretive work.

Opposite right

This is the long gone Taunton Monument and New Walk, which was originally a continuation of The Plains. Wm. Doidge Taunton was Mayor in 1824. During his Mayoralty a pleasure ground and Bowling Green was opened and a plaque on the feature known as the Taunton Monument read: "This Walk is dedicated to the Public by the Corporation of Totnes, William D. Taunton, Mayor". Alas the monument was demolished in the mid 1950s. The New Walk had an avenue of chestnut trees which were planted during the Mayoralty of Dr. Roger Birdwood, who was thrice Mayor in 1781, 1789 and 1795.

Right

A traffic jam in the Narrows before 1928, nothing changes!

On 14 February 1968 the first meeting to form a 'Girls Choir' was held and the outcome was 'The Music Makers'. The idea to form such a choir came from Harold Tomlins (the deputy organist, of Totnes Methodist Church). Mrs Betty Southern suggested a distinctive uniform and not only did she raise the money for the material needed but she also made all the outfits herself. For some years the Choir performed to help charities. The photo shows Harold Tomlins and Betty Southern with the choir presenting a concert at the Civic Hall in aid of the National Children's Homes on 15 December 1974.

The Totnes Amateur Operatic and Dramatic Society's first production was in 1937 - "The Pirates of Penzance". For many years the Society annually produced a 'Gilbert & Sullivan' opera and also two plays. This picture shows the 1949 production of Oscar Wilde's "Lady Windermere's Fan". The cast included Geraldine Massey, Bernard and Ivy Reed, Marjorie Todd, Joseph Smith, Joy Gawne, Peter Budd, Nellie Doidge, Lawson Lean, Archie Steel, Geoffrey Hellings and Bill Bennett. Totnes has been entertained by 'Totnesians' over the centuries - there are recorded references to the plays acted by the 'boys of Totnes' when they performed at Dartmouth and Plymouth in the 16th century.

Food parcels from America during the War and just after were always gratefully received. Here members of the Totnes old Folks Club receive parcels from the Mayor and Mayoress Cllr. Frank Rowe and his wife. Members include well known characters such as Granny Rellands, Mrs Howis and Jack Brown.

The 'Harbourne Singers' were founded in 1966 to promote the 'sheer joy of singing' - the founder members being Gordon Brown (Totnes Parish Church organist), Michael Griffiths, Paul Irwin, and the Rev. Michael Malsom, Vicar of Harberton). Their works over the year to the present day include Handel's "Messiah", Edw. German's "Merrie England", Gilbert & Sullivan's "Mikado" and "Pirates of Penzance" (concert versions), and Christmas cantatas. These concerts have been performed in various churches and halls and under the direction of various musical directors. This is a photograph of "Merrie England" (1969) in the Civic Hall, Totnes. The Musical Direction was by Gordon Brown, with Accompanist Dorothy Mineard and Soloists (L to R) Michael Mingo, Pamela Cleave, Gordon Brown, Joan Ashby and Howard Pickard.

This is Cistern Street (formerly known as Harper's Hill Street). The house with the hanging washing (No 10) was granted by the will of Chas. Taylor (1734) to form part of the Totnes Charity School Foundation - the poor children were to be provided on admission with books clothes and apparel. In the 19th century the clothes were changed from mainly grey serge to blue with brass buttons and became known as the Blue Coat School. With the spread of elementary education from the mid 19th century the need for the Charity School declined and it was closed in 1890.

The Leechwells consist of three stone baths or sinks, fed by three jets of water coming out of holes in an adjacent wall. Wardens of the Lychewylle were appointed in the Middle Ages and the names of those between 1405 - 1475 are known. In 1670 Wm. Alford was paid £5.50 for repairing the Leechwell. In Lyson's "Magna Britannia" of 1665 a medical spring is mentioned and this probably refers to the wells. The troughs were known locally as The Snake, the Toad and the Long Crippler (grass snake). Mr E. Windeatt wrote in 1894 -"one spring was considered efficacious to relieve diseased eyes and is still used, the centre trough helped with the bite of a grass snake and the other trough helped to ease skin disease".

Early in this century the General Post Office was at No 1 Fore Street. In 1914 it moved to No 27 Fore Street which had a beautiful walled garden and the Postmaster lived on the premises. However, in the mid 1920s the GPO decided that larger premises were needed so bought No 25 and 23. The Post Office moved out of No 27 which was bought by H.G. (Joe) Tapley who had previously run a cinema in the Ballroom of the Seven Stars Hotel. He turned No 27 into a modern cinema, the first film shown was "Dark Red Roses". During World War II the cinema was gutted by fire. (Back row L to R) Messrs. Setters, Bow, Phillips, Poolman, Tucker, Perring, Tapley, Setters, Matters, Stoyle, Hocking, L. Taylor, Sercombe, Boroden, Yeoman, Cotten, Soper, E. Barrett, Horswill, Dennis, Perony and T. Carter. (Front row L to R) Miss Collom, A. Parnell, Miss Strickland, A.F. Knott (second in command), A.E. Birkett (Head Postmaster), R.H. Gill (Postmaster, South Brent), Miss J. House, A.J. Glover and Miss M. Edmonds.